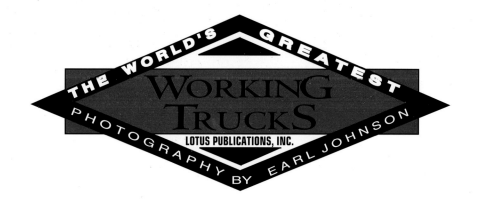

A LOTUS PUBLICATIONS FINE BOOK

The World's Greatest Working Trucks
Photography by Earl L. Johnson  Written by Grace M. Hawkins
Volume I • May 1997
Printed in Hong Kong

ISBN 0-9649645-4-6

Dedication

My professional career owes as much to the work of my wife, Grace Hawkins, as it does to my own efforts. Without her constant encouragement, criticism, and support personally and in our business, this book would not have been possible. I couldn't get her to take a bow anywhere but here, and she agreed to this dedication only after I pointed out that there is hardly a company in these pages (or perhaps anywhere) which has not had an insufficiently acknowledged partner in its success. Usually, it's the wife who attends not only to all the thousands of details that civilize us, but also somehow finds seemingly limitless energy for the business as well. By including all these wives and business partners in this Dedication, I persuaded Grace to agree to include it in this volume. So, please, take a bow, and thank you from the bottom of my heart.

Lotus Publications, Inc.
P.O. Box 4452
South Colby, WA 98384

Visit Us On The World Wide Web at http://lotuspub.com
e-mail: lotus111@ix.netcom.com

How The Idea Came About

During the 13 months spent doing research and photography for The World's Greatest Working Trucks, many people asked where the idea for this book arose from. Why trucks? Where did the interest come from? The answer is both simple and complex, because the book started the way most ideas do, as a flight of the imagination. Something that might be possible, and might not.

As time went by, the more the idea was discussed the more it took hold and gathered speed. Soon it was no longer a question of whether to embark on the book's production, but how

soon and what part of the country would offer the most interesting trucks.

Earl Johnson's photography has been published many times before in various magazines as well as in three collections. Two of these are now out of print, and the third is still widely available in various bookstores. That book, The World's Greatest Tow Trucks, proved that the general public is interested in tow trucks — and not just on a cold night when the car keys are locked in the trunk. Also, much of the interest

undoubtedly stems from the beautiful scenery captured in the
photographs

The tow trucks are everything
from $350,000 one-of-a-kind rotators
to light duty show trucks, and the
backgrounds range from the Eiffel
Tower in Paris to the crystal clear
skyline of San Francisco. Still,
everyone was surprised by the
interest shown in such a specific
type of equipment.

Encouraged by the popularity
of that recent book, a project which
would range more widely over the
many types of trucks in use today
began to take shape. It's a rare
person who can see a big truck,
almost any big truck, go by on the

highway without a glance in its
direction. When that truck is
dressed up with any of the many
special effects on the market today
it's certain to turn heads. The
onlooker wonders where it's headed,
what cargo it carries, who the driver
is and what that restless life is like.
Then, headed from work to home or
home to work along the same daily
path, confined within the predictable
routines of most modern lives, a stab
of jealousy or a moment of wander-
lust comes to the surface.

The truck represents unlimited
horizons. It's going farther in a
week than many people will in a
year. It might drive millions of miles
before its life is over. In thousands
of songs, trucks carry a weighted

message of faithless lovers, twin longings for home and freedom, romance and endlessly repeating double white lines. Everyone listens to these songs, not just truck drivers. The words speak to us of searching and escaping, and the music always has a relentless rhythm mocking the turning of eighteen tires mile after mile.

Manufacturers induce us to buy their make and model by photographing the trucks with glamorous models in evening dress. Sometimes the shots are taken at sunrise to capture the endless 24 hour travel cycle a truck is built to handle. The images are seldom ordinary because they are meant to underscore the mystery and power of the product the ads are selling: the truck.

The truck has totally invaded all levels of society. The biggest profit area for Ford and General Motors in the early years of the 1990's is the light duty truck. Even the latest "I made it" status symbol for the suburban family, a $35,000 four wheel drive vehicle, was a truck. It's an expensive truck, but it's still a truck.

So the time had come for a book focused on the working truck. Over the months needed to shoot this book, the publishers met many of the people who

People And Their Trucks

make these working trucks go. The more time we spent, the more interesting stories they revealed.

This photo of Steve Rodgerson was taken at an antique truck show and captures the character of the former rodeo cowboy who took up the challenge one day when a disgusted tow truck owner remarked, "I hate this business; here, take the keys to this truck." Within two years, Steve had built Technique Towing into Fresno's major player. He thinks of it as a people service business, and aims to give the best service. And he loves his trucks, too.

All the trucks in this book are respected, lovingly cared for, given names, and fall just short of being worshipped. The meticulous maintenance they are subjected to is an important component of their profitability. A broken-down truck isn't making anyone any money. And the investment represented by any one of these power units is substantial, so it must be protected. There is more going on than cold-hearted financial calculation in these trucks, however, and the owners and drivers would be the first to admit it.

The mural under the smiling face in this photo is one of a pair, the other mural showing this double bulk trailer on a different stretch of road, swinging its full seventy-five foot length through hair-pin turns on the Pacific Coast Highway with a no-sweat nonchalance that's hard to believe if you've ever driven those roads. The owner, Bill Hay, always has the same artist paint new door panel murals for his trucks. Each one is unique, extraordinarily detailed, and accented with gold. These murals and the other accents lavished on all the family's trucks (see page 86) don't improve performance, but they contribute powerfully to the company/family/business in other ways.

All rules or generalities have exceptions and that holds true in these pages. It is safe to say, nevertheless, that a profile of people in this book is as follows. A driving entrepreneurial force (in this photo is Bob Pearce of Phoenix, AZ) bursts out of high school

or the military, fed up to the teeth with regimentation and boredom. Cobbling together some money from somewhere, a truck is bought. Usually right about now a woman enters the picture and on top of the usual occupations her talents are turned to paying bills, sending out invoices, and answering the phone—in between changing diapers and tucking in shirttails for church on Sunday.

The children grow up with hearing the phones ring at all hours of the day and night and can back up an eighteen wheeler at age 11, in the yard only of course. There is plenty of work to go around because the company is growing despite the increasing complexity of the transportation industry in America, but the kids stay in school longer than the parents, often graduating from college and returning

to the family business in time to bring it to the next level. Even if they wanted to escape it, how could they? And besides, it's both fun and cool.

Monsieur Michelin in this photo isn't full of air. He's held up on the inside by Alex Lorenz, son of Sound Tire's Kim Lorenz. Alex was 13 when this photo was taken at the picnic where Sound Tire's photo session was done. Of course we can't choose our parents, but isn't it much more fun to have a Dad who has a Monsieur Michelin outfit at a giant retread facility, or one who drives a glorious chromed-out Kenworth, rather than, say, a Dad whose title is "consultant"? Where's the romance in something like that?

The kids know what their parents do all day, and during school vacations they pitch in too. In spite of the strains and stresses any family business is bound to experience, most families make the necessary accommodations and the enterprise continues to grow. In those cases where there are just too many powerful temperaments colliding, the end result is often positive too: a new business venture is created by the

nail that just couldn't be pounded down. That's business in America!

So the kids are involved, and not just the kids, the grandchildren too. The third generation in this close-up of page 38 is only 5 and 2 years old, the grandchildren of Joel and Carole Olson—-and we're all counting on them to take the reins in their turn. How else will all the goods and commodities we rely on be delivered to our homes and businesses? The very long-term future for the trucking industry has never been stronger, rumors to the contrary. Like magazines, which are thriving in spite of the predictions twenty years ago that computers would put them out of business, and like newspapers which are under similar future shock predictions, trucking companies will be needed for a long time and have nothing to fear from technological advances.

The owners of the businesses in this book do more than run their own shop. Like Bob Berry of Oakland, CA, shown here in front of one of his favorites, they often give large amounts of their time to the industry they work in. Not content to help themselves, they help their competitors too. Not busy enough with everyday headaches in their own backyards, they take on those of the county, state and even country.

Investing a year as President of a state association, as many of the people in this book have, is no small undertaking. It means not only putting aside the daily concerns of the enterprise that sustains the business and of course the family, but developing the hide of a rhinoceros and the antennae of a butterfly. For some reason, appreciation is not always overwhelming, or so it seems at the time. Old rivalries re-emerge, eyes are narrowed at the advantages to be had from being close to power, and all points of view cannot prevail simultaneously. Harry Truman

said of the social climate of Washington, DC., "If you want a friend, get a dog." In spite of the trials, people step forward and in doing so move their industry forward.

The time contributed to their states notwithstanding, there is a leftover reserve of passionate enthusiasm also for a combination of history and hobby: preserving the trucks of the past. Ed Rocha, a California Trucking Association Past President, shown here

strolling past his own prize-winning 1924 1-ton Model T at the antique show that Terry puts on every year in Fresno, is also on the Board of the Hays Antique Truck Museum (see page 21), as are others in these pages. Terry Fortier's interest is so strong that

he has created a museum himself. He himself has served in the post of President of C.T.A., as has his brother Tim in 1996-97.

All work and no play would mean a dull group of people. No worries about that

here! In this photo, Earl captured Lloyd Farmer of Valley Materials on his Harley Davidson. Plenty of these newly-respectable motorcycles sparkle in the back garages of trucking companies. When they're not polishing trucks for Beauty Contests, our companies pursue interests from flying vintage crop dusters to raising sled dogs.

Standing in front of one of their signature red Peterbilts against the snowy Grand Tetons is 1997-1998 Chairman of the Idaho Trucking Council Heber Andrus and his brother, Doug. Doug covers when Heber is on Council or University business, and

Heber steps in when Doug's extra-office duties take him away from his desk. It's a partnership they've had since both can remember, and the staff team at Doug Andrus Distributing functions seamlessly even when one brother or another is away on community business.

All the owners representing the trucks in this book were, or are, drivers first. Regardless of how often they get behind the wheel now, they seem to remember clearly the importance of the driver's comfort and safety. A success-ful fleet doesn't drive itself, and to find, train and retain a high quality of driver is every company's top priority. Drive around the back of any truck stop, and you'll see drivers attending to their trucks as if they owned them themselves. Their employers understand that well-outfitted trucks attract the kind of driver who will both take care of the valuable investment and deliver the kind of dedication the owner once delivered.

In this photo is Jorge Guererro, a top driver for Freddie Mac's (see page 73). Uniformed, crisp in the hot California sun, Jorge is the face of the

company to every tow he performs every day. When a truck and operator like this arrives on the scene of a disablement, accident or even a routine setting job, everyone relaxes; they know they're in good hands.

How did Earl Johnson get all these photos? If you really want to know, all you have to do is ask. He's always willing to give tips to onlookers or amateur shooters. One of the pages in this book was even taken under his long distance direction when a truck was simply unavailable at the time of the shoot. See pages 56 and 57 and see if you can tell which one he shot and which one Manager Scott Palmer took using

the film and instructions Earl gave. Both instructor and pupil did a good job, don't you agree?

The photographs in this book were all taken with much care, a good deal of stomping around and fretting (several pairs of cowboy boots wore out), phenomenal good fortune with weather conditions and terrific cooperation from the owners of the equipment. To get the angles and locations was easy; Earl just had to be willing to have himself shot out on the end of a hydraulic boom or lifted in a shovel, as these two photos show. He had to be willing to get poison oak scrambling up a California hillside to

the only spot from which a certain shot could be had.

On occasions too numerous to mention, he's had cordial but tense discussions with various representatives of what Texans call The Law. Somehow, after generous expressions of regret for any inconvenience, firm promises to leave right after this shot without delay, and even long explanations about the importance of the book to the trucking industry, the concerned authorities always relented. Some are even on a list to be sent copies of the book upon publication. A few have been photographed posing proudly next to the truck they came to evict with all the righteousness of their authority.

Waiting, waiting, waiting is another component of getting the shots in this book, as it is with any photography. Wildlife photographers endure miseries of weather, insects and no-show quarry. Working on a project such as this one meant shooting around the busy schedules of the companies. These are not show trucks, or the garaged pets of their owners. They all have to earn their keep everyday, and their schedules are complex. On those occasions when tight schedules did not allow for the truck or fleet to be moved far, Earl had to scout last minute alterna-

tive locations which still showed off the truck to maximum advantage.

Things can go wrong. One truck had a bumper crunched the day before the shoot and required Earl to drive 750 miles round trip to shoot it later. His fingers were so cold during one shoot and the wind was howling so loudly that he wasn't sure the camera was firing. It wouldn't have been fun to go back and try to do it again, and it wasn't necessary, but at the time it was a nagging worry.

After the shots were done for each company, the film was consigned to express delivery to our offices, which during this project made a small move around the corner from New York State to Washington State. Until each page's processed negatives, proofs and slides were returned to our files from the lab and checked by Earl, there was always the remote possibility of loss or technical problems. None occurred.

This volume did not involve going back and forth to Europe and is centered on the western states, so Earl did not travel as many miles as he did for his last book, <u>The World's Greatest Tow Trucks</u>. That volume clocked up 20,000 miles in nine short months. This volume did keep him away from home from January 1996 until August in one long stretch, however, and then again until November. It's the same with most work people do; it may look like an easy way to make a living until you really get down to the nuts and bolts. Suddenly you realize that you have to love it to do it.

Back at the Lotus Publication offices, where the collating, calling, faxing and e-mailing of information takes place, the post-production went on while Earl was out getting all the images. Ably assisted by the company greyhound, Cajun, the book was put together by our Staff, Stacey Quinn, Carmen Babcock, Hannah Hawkins, and me, Grace. We had editorial assistance from Dee Johnson, and nothing but interference from the company cat

Bumper who likes to lick the surface of photographs.

The book itself would not have been possible, when all factors are taken into account, without the encouragement of several people we mention here by name and many others who remarked, "Hey, that's a great idea for a book!" but whose names we never knew or happened to forget. The names we remember are Mike Lorentzen, Terry Fortier, Diana Greever, Pete Carr, Victor Villard, George Weaver, Butch Weir, Bill Robertson, Steve Rodgerson, Don and Arlene Redfearn and Shirley and Tom Micarelli. To those we fail to include, and it's certain there are some important ones, thanks and we regret not mentioning you.

Most of all, a thank you to all the companies who participated with us in this book. It was a pleasure working with you all and your cooperation and patience has born fruit in this project as it has with so many others you've undertaken in your careers. It's your book.

Grace and Earl
February, 1997

Kings County Truck Lines, whose general office is in Tulare, California, recently celebrated 56 years of service to the industry. Founded by the late Manuel S. "Spike" Mancebo in 1940, his son, Manuel Mancebo, Jr., is president and CEO and has been at the helm since 1971. "J.R." Mancebo is dedicated to offering quality service, quality equipment, quality personnel and quality maintenance, the ingredients that comprise KCTL's motto: "Quality is Kings County Truck Lines." KCTL serves the western states with terminals strategically located in California, Nevada and Oregon.

Pictured are examples of the late model quality equipment KCTL offers: 3-axle conventional Freightliner tractors, insulated and dry utility vans, and food-grade insulated stainless steel Westmark tankers. The reefer van shown is one highly spec'd for KCTL to specialize in transporting ice cream and other deep frozen commodities.

Berkeley Concrete Pumping, Inc. (BCP) is located in Berkeley, California, near the Golden Gate Bridge shown here. The company services the Northern California construction industry with 40 of the most advanced concrete pumps available since 1979. Berkeley Concrete Pumping's fleet of booms range in length from the 23 meter (75 ft.) to the longest and fastest concrete pump in North America, the 52 meter (171 ft.). Added to the ever-growing fleet is the BPL 1200 HDR 23/125 KVM 42 meter concrete pump pictured here, mounted on a MR 688S truck. This pump will reach out to 138 feet and pump concrete at the rate of 170 cubic yards per hour.

The evolution of the Schwing line of concrete pumps has resulted in Berkeley Concrete Pumping, Inc. having the broadest line of concrete pumps available in the construction industry. When concrete is a major factor in a job's profit margin, you need companies that support what they promise. Berkeley Concrete Pumping, Inc. and Schwing America are such companies.

In 1982, an enterprising young man spotted what seemed to be a unique opportunity: providing high profile, image-conscious customers with responsible handling of the hazardous wastes generated by their businesses. Black Gold's Victor Villard reasoned that he could win and keep the best customers by providing not just good service but outstandingly beautiful trucks. The two units shown with removeable tanks are unique in the industry, built to Victor's specifications and shown here against Lake Casitas from Vista Point in Ventura County, California.

Today 14 shining black and gold International trucks perform their hauling, cleaning, and transport services to a wide variety of happy customers, among them government agencies, printing shops, farms, major chain stores and high tech companies. Part of the new wave of reuse, recycle and renew, Victor's fleet busies itself shuttling between its customers and recycling companies or users of alternative fuels: a true model of the future. And when the fleet is not on the road, it's out back at the Ventura location being polished up for tomorrow's work.

Double Eagle Transportation was started by Jerry Butcher in May, 1992 with big hopes and dreams for the future. Putting six trucks and six drivers with "winning attitudes" on the road, the company was on its way. Now based in Fontana, California, this bulk commodity carrier hauling cement-related products has customers that range in location from the Mexican border to Bakersfield to Las Vegas... wherever they are needed!

Double Eagle prides itself by treating people the way people want to be treated. Jerry says, "Give the drivers a truck they can be proud of, and they will be." From the first six drivers who stuck through the hard times to the new drivers coming in later, it's their winning attitudes and their team work that enables Double Eagle to provide their customers with the best possible service. Four years later, Jerry's philosophy is proving itself. Double Eagle is still growing, with a current count of 27 trucks and 40 employees.

This Pierce Arrow lumber truck and Ralston Trailer was used to haul lumber from the Spaulding Lumber Company in Converse Basin to Fresno California (Converse Basin is located near the Sequoia National Park). The truck and trailer combination had brakes on one axle. Air shocks on the front spring suspension allowed the driver to adjust the pressure according to riding comfort. Because of the solid rubber tires, the suspension was not much help!

The truck was restored by Don L. Hays at the Hays Antique Truck Museum in Woodland, California, about 1980.

Paso Robles Truck Center calls the beautiful California Central Coast home. They were established in the early 1960's and are now a full service truck dealership. Owners since 1983, Stan and Steve Ormonde oversee a team operation that includes sales, service, parts, towing, body and paint. Housed on Highway 46, they provide services on this main artery that connects both coasts.

Their highly trained staff, using state of the art equipment, continue to provide the best possible service available to a diversified customer base. Currently operating 3 heavy duty tow trucks, the "Bro" shown here was completely built on the premises by their employees. Another example of quality designed by Paso Robles Truck Center.

In 1975, after Tom Micarelli had worked 5 years for his trucking company, he and Shirley Micarelli had an option to purchase the truck he had been driving and lease it back to the company. Then, in November, 1976, they decided to go completely on their own. Presently based in the town of Fillmore, they still continue to service their original customers: farmers and a large egg ranch. They are now also doing soil amendment hauling for the local orchards and vineyards of Santa Barbara and San Luis Obispo counties. They still have their original 1974, two 1988 T-800s and a 1989 W-900 series (all 2 axle) and then their special 960 Kenworth which they hold much pride in, but then they have pride in all their equipment. They plan to maintain what they have and hope that their grandchildren will become involved, as their children have. Tom and Shirley are active in the California Trucking Association and in their community. Micarelli's has received safety awards from the CTA and insurance companies. Last but not least, past and present their employees have helped them accomplish what they have become as a company. To each they express their sincere appreciation and thanks.

Harris Ranch of Coalinga, California: 1995 Freightliner Beef Truck (Below): The 1995 Freightliner is set up with a 365 HP Detroit engine geared for economical highway travel and top speed controlled by the engine computer. It is equipped with modern hi-tech temperature control capable of maintaining the ultimate ambient to protect the integrity and quality of the finished product. Travelling the full length of the state of California, the truck encounters the searing heat of the valley and the freezing cold of the mountains. The high quality beef is delivered to top quality meat suppliers and the best restaurants in the state of California, such as the Harris Ranch Restaurant and Inn located on I-5 in central California, also known as an oasis. Harris Ranch Beef operates 38 trucks to deliver the finished product.

1995 Freightliner Cattle Truck (Opposite Page): Equipped with a Detroit 430 HP engine, this truck has non-slip locking differentials and is geared so that it can traverse the unimproved roads of western ranches. This truck makes it possible for ranchers to utilize rugged and mountainous country that otherwise would be non-productive. By being able to move cattle in and out of this rough dry country, ranchers can better manage delicate rangeland, making for a well-balanced yet productive ecosystem. Wildlife, as well as livestock, can thus co-exist without damaging the environment. Over the western highways of the United States, with their computer-controlled road speed, the trucks are an invaluable tool for the beef and dairy industry.

Harris pioneered beef shipping to the Orient. First on the hoof, the cattle are loaded from the livestock trucks onto 747 airplanes. Today, the specially fed and processed beef is delivered to international airports for overseas shipments. The trucks are set up to handle either the modern boxed beef or the old-fashioned hanging beef. Either way, the consumer gets the best quality finished product. Beef--it's what's for dinner!

What began modestly in 1937 on the westside of California's San Joachim Valley today has become the stuff of western legend...Harris Ranch. Harris Ranch has grown since the early days into one of California's largest farming operations as well as California's largest cattle feeder and fed beef processor. Today, Harris Ranch is a fully-intergrated company consisting of Harris Farms, Harris Feeding Company, Harris Ranch Beef Company, Harris Ranch Horse Division as well as the world-famous Harris Ranch Restaurant and Inn. Beef processed by Harris Ranch Beef Company is marketed throughout the West as well as internationally.

Distinguished by an emphasis on a quality work environment and employee loyalty, Bill & Wags started, as owners Bill and Rita Robertson say, "on no money and a lot of hope." Their first truck, a Willys with a slide-in Zenith boom and electric winch, is still stored in their all new 3-acre yard for old times sake. Located 45 miles east of Los Angeles in Southern California, between Interstate 10 and Interstate 60, their customers range from local retail and commercial customers to national carriers—all depending on swift careful handling from Bill & Wags' experienced staff. The company's goal is to be the best, with the best equipment and facilities—not necessarily the largest. Continuing a tradition of slow steady growth while continuing to give back to its community, Bill & Wags fosters a pleasant workplace with good compensation, insurance, profit sharing and paid vacations. The resulting employee retention rate has been a major factor in the company's long years of success.

On The Cover

Kelvin Hildebrand Trucking of Watsonville, California presents the fourth generation of trucking history: Jane, age 7, Macie, age 5, and Hanna, three years old. Baby Joseph missed being in the photo by a few days. Between their uncle Theron Hildebrand's company and their Dad's, the family companies can field 100 power units and 150 sets of trailers. Hauling mainly sand and gravel construction materials with transfers, bottom dumps and end dumps, the companies serve Central and Northern California. The brothers also assist in the operation of the company owned by their aunt, Morya Gularte Trucking. The first generation, Jim Hildebrand, bought his first truck in 1945, and passed on the reins to his son James T. who died in 1980 at the young age of 40. *This page is dedicated to James Hildebrand, James T. Hildebrand, and James B. Hildebrand, Kelvin's late brother.*

Commercial Transfer Inc., (CTI) is a California-based truck load carrier. This line is owned and operated by Terry and Tim Fortier. The Fortier family bought Commercial Transfer in the early 1930's and merged it into Fortier Transportation Company until 1960, when the parent company was sold. The Commercial Transfer name was reactivated by Russell and Terry Fortier and incorporated by them in 1963. CTI has operated continuously since then with 50 power units and over 140 trailers throughout California and the eleven western states. The trailer fleet consists of flatbeds, vans, curtainsides, and pneumatic equipment. The inset photo shows Terry Fortier's beautifully restored 1952 Kenworth. Representing the third generation in the freight hauling business, Terry and Tim have both served as president of the California Trucking Association.

Continued On Next Page

Continued From Previous Page

Their grandfather used horses and drayage wagons in 1911.

This family-owned business prides itself on service and appearance as well as its commitment to the use of the most current technology -- such as satellite communication, on-board computers with electronic logs, prepass -- available. Above is a 1998 Volvo "VN" series 3-axle tractor with 1997 J&L 1200 cubic feet pneumatic semi trailer. The page to the left shows a 1997 Freightliner cabover 2 axle tractor with a set of 28 1/2' by 102" Utility "Tautliner" curtainside trailers. The CTI terminal in Fresno houses a museum of Western Carriers memorabilia as well as a collection of antique trucks.

Sward Trucking, Inc. was started in 1966 by Vic and Gail Sward and is located on 18 acres in the Oakdale countryside (equidistant from San Francisco, Sacramento and Fresno). Although their primary traffic lanes are between Arizona, California, Nevada, Oregon and Washington, the majority of their daily traffic is between Northern and Southern California. They believe that the ability to transport a wide range of general as well as specialty commodities is essential to serving the needs of their customers. Among the commodities they transport in truckload quantities are lumber, roofing, insulation and related building materials, corrugated paper, waste paper, glass containers, empty cans, plastic bottles, case goods and plastic pipe.

The majority of Sward Trucking's business is handled by their 52 tractors and 95 trailing units, with the balance made up by qualified owner-operators and subhaulers. They take great pride in offering overnight delivery service to most points in California. They are also proud of their excellent safety record since their founding in 1966, and have been given a safety award by the Califonia Trucking Association.

B&B Red-I-Mix Concrete, Inc. was started on February 1, 1961, by Bill Thomas and Bill Cleveland, hence the name B&B. Mal Gatherer, Bill Thomas' son-in-law, became a partner in 1970. In 1978, Bill Thomas decided to retire at the age of 76 and Mal became sole owner. On January 1, 1996, Mal decided to retire and passed the torch to his son Mike.

B&B Red-I-Mix Concrete is located in the northeast San Gabriel Valley and serves the entire San Gabriel Valley, primarily focusing on small contractors and homeowners. They are a family owned business where all 20 employees are treated as family members. Everyone works hard and takes great pride in giving their customers the quality service and product that they stake their reputation on.

Valley Materials of Stockton, California, was started in 1984 by Lloyd Farmer (l.) and Phil Muller (r.). They specialize in hauling overlength lumber, laminated beams and concrete roof tile using all air ride equipment and operating over a range of 7 western states. Steady growth over the last ten years has resulted in a fleet size of 60 trucks, and the company plans to keep right on growing. The Valley Materials motto is "Commitment to Excellence in Service."

Mid-State Truck and Rigging, Inc. introduced the first mobile cranes to Phoenix back in the days when the population of this booming city was under 50,000. Today, on a daily basis, Mid-State handles manufacturing equipment for aerospace, electronics industries, nuclear power plants, construction firms, and many other military and civilian related equipment. The firm's founder, Elvis Baker, remains a strong anchor with son, Dick, and a third generation presently in college preparing to continue the company's course. The power units are all Macks and the several hundred auxiliarypieces of equipment range from forklifts with 4,000 lb to 90,000 lb capacity and truck and trailer combinations of up to 100 tons. There is no job too unusual or too tough for the experienced professionals at Mid-State...guaranteed!

Doug Andrus Distributing, Inc. is a family owned company located in Idaho Falls, Idaho. The company operates mainly Peterbilt tractors powered by 436 Cummins, Cat and Detroit engines pulling Utility and Western trailers. The operations cover the entire 48 states with half the equipment hauling temperature controlled freight and the remainder of the equipment hauling flatbed and bulk commodities. The tractors are traded every 3-1/2 years to take full advantage of new engines and drive train technologies. Doug Andrus drivers enjoy simply the best equipment on the road today.

In the spring of 1937, Doug Andrus began trucking with a 1935 Chevrolet truck. He hauled coal from the mines in Wyoming to the residences of eastern Idaho. The following year, Doug turned to hauling grain to the dairymen of Utah and

Continued On Next Page

Continued From Previous Page

coal to eastern Idaho from the coal mines of Utah. At age 32, Doug was a hard worker, very ambitious and desired only to make a good living for his family and those who worked with him. His best attributes were his honesty and integrity. Doug carried his great reputation wherever he went. Like every family-owned business, his sons and daughters were soon included in the work and all learned to drive trucks at an early age.

When Doug retired in 1975, he turned the management of the company over to his sons, Doug Jr. and Heber Andrus. Doug Jr. and Heber are graduates of Brigham Young University. Both young men drove trucks to get them through their college years and enjoyed the industry enough to make it their lifelong vocational pursuit. Doug Jr. and Heber have built the company from six trucks in 1975 to its present size of 155 power units and 255 trailers. Both attribute their success to their dedicated employees, their loyal customers, and supportive suppliers and associates.

In 1997, Doug Andrus Distributing, Inc. celebrates 60 years of trucking on America's highways and is looking forward to many successful and productive years ahead.

Joel Olson Trucking is known throughout the Pacific Northwest for a stunning fleet specialized for forest products transportation. Joel's first rigs as he exited high school were humble dump trucks, but his eye soon noticed the growth in log trucking, and the first log truck he bought was followed quickly by three more. As time went by, demand fueled regular increases in the fleet. Customer requests from lumber companies such as RSG Forest Products necessitated a flatbed fleet and then a new opportunity came along. Logging landings presented a constant debris problem to the logging companies as well as to the forest managers. The Olson solution was to have large drop boxes on site to collect the waste material, which quickly became a viable operation on its own. Corporate accounts such as Longview Fibre and Weyerhaeuser busy the fleet of 15 trucks and over 200 boxes. Material once burned or discarded is now put to use, a boon to customers and the environment alike.

Continued On Next Page

Joel Olson Trucking is a family operation, with all members active in the forest industry. Darin Olson is the General Manager and has 4 trucks of his own. Son Craig is a forest engineer. Grandchildren, our third generation, include Darin's Anndres and Alex and Craig's Kaprice and Kody. The Oregon headquarters also house the real boss, Oscar the dachshund.

Ganduglia Trucking was started in 1939 by Vincent Ganduglia. Located in Fresno, California, one of the most productive areas of the entire US, the company is perfectly situated to service the agriculture industry as well as the manufacturing industry statewide. Its range of equipment includes flatbeds, drop decks, pneumatic, stainless, self-unloading and oil spreading trucks. All equipment is capable of hauling 50,000 to 57,000 lb. and the company purchases the most technologically advanced equipment on the market as a method of maintaining peak operating efficiency. The Staff at Ganduglia is composed of 48 dedicated drivers, 6 office and 11 shop personnel. The company presently operates 48 power units and 100 trailers and is managed by the second generation of Vincent Ganduglia's family.

West Coast Sand and Gravel of Buena Park, California, started in 1968. The first Struiksma generation retired, leaving a growing enterprise to the three brothers, Marvin, Bob and John, who operate the company now. Hauling sand and gravel has produced a 53-truck 379 Peterbilt fleet with Cummins M11, 330 HP with 10-speed transmissions and Superior boxes. Most trucks work in the Los Angeles basin, but customer needs sometimes take them farther. Ten trucks are stationed in the Oakdale location. Fifty of the trucks are transfers, two are ten-wheelers, and one is an end dump. The third generation, Dale, Mike and Jeff Struiksma, are involved now, and the company's success seems assured as the team continues to balance the extra effort required for growth with a harmonious family enterprise.

Resource Building Materials, Inc. operates a supply source for every kind of building material imaginable from bricks to sand and gravel to tools from three locations in California, Stanton, City of Industry, and Chino. Each yard's individual manager has on hand carefully spec'd and well-maintained straight delivery trucks such as the one in the photo to deliver commercial quantity loads and smaller 2-axle trucks for residential supply. From these three locations, Resource Materials services all of Southern California and, from its start in 1988, has continued to grow through the ups and downs of the market.

Payton Trucking, Inc. specializes in the transport of commercial modular/mobile buildings throughout the western United States. Founded nearly 20 years ago as a family enterprise by Eugene Payton, it remains one today operated by sons Tom and Carl in Tulare, CA. The small fleet of trucks shows the pride they have in their equipment, some of the finest "toters" on the road. The company motto of "Leading The Way, Doing It Right" illustrates their commitment to provide only "Quality Service." The company operates various types of equipment to meet changing needs, all equipped with air ride suspension which greatly reduces road stress fractures to the buildings. They utilize state of the art communication systems with radio, cellular phone and paging capabilities to maintain flexibility in load changes. The company plans to continue on a moderate growth path, adding more low boy capabilities that will allow them to remain "Simply the Best" in their unique niche market.

Maggini Hay of Riverdale, California, got its start when the owner, Melvin Maggini, bought an old truck at age 16 and announced to his Dad that it was his life's ambition to haul hay. For the next 11 years he did exactly that for a broker, and when the gentleman died in 1976, he began buying and selling hay himself. By then he and his wife Jessie had not only a thriving business but two daughters, Annette and Barbara, who today work in the office, and son, Mike, who owns the hay squeeze pictured here, a '96 Peterbilt with a 475 Caterpillar engine, 10 speed transmission and SQ-100 rear ends plus a 27 1/2 ' bed and 30' pull trailer. For recreation, the family often enters truck contests, and first place trophies decorate their Riverdale office.

The advanced electronics of MEGADUMP are the latest in a line of innovative equipment and services provided by this long established company owned by Randy Hastie. Randy's father Bill started the company in 1941 with his wife Nancy. The company was instrumental in the rebuilding of Sacramento after the floods of the 50's, and in constructing the runways of Mather Air Force Base and the new freeways of the 60's.

Under Randy's leadership in the early 70's, a new era of growth resulted from the introduction of a retail operation geared towards many new rock and soil products custom blended onsite. The trucking end of the business has evolved to over 30 units of varying sizes catering to anything from small homeowners to the largest construction jobs. The trucks' distinctive chromed red and green color schemes have been landmarks of quality and service in the Sacramento area for 55 years.

MP Environmental Services, Inc. is a family owned and operated business. Founded in 1942 by Mitchell Pecarovich (the "MP"), the Company is run today by his daughter and son-in-law, Dawn and David Calderwood. M P Environmental Services operates one of the largest independent fleets in the Western US dedicated to the transportation of hazardous wastes. Offices in Bakersfield, Woodland and Azusa, CA., Phoenix, AZ and Seattle, WA serve customers ranging from the corner gas station to the Departments of Energy and Defense. A wide variety of quality equipment, including roll-offs, vacuum trucks, dump trucks and vans, coupled with a team of highly skilled drivers, has allowed M P Environmental Services, Inc. to establish itself as one of the premier hazardous waste transportation companies in the West.

Great America Towing and Transportation is located in San Jose, California, the center of America's computer industry. Suitably, Great America Towing offers its commercial and private clients the same high level of technological advances in its state-of-the-art towing equipment. Established by current owner Dino Tomassi's late father, Angelo Tomassi, Sr. in 1973, Great America has grown to a fleet of over 50 pieces of equipment able to handle any situation that might arise. Our light duty division can handle any car, boat or motorcycle. Our car carriers can handle exotic cars and hard-to-tow vehicles and equipment. Our heavy duty under reach trucks tow buses, tractor trailers, tankers and do major recoveries and rollovers in conjunction with our air cushion recovery service. The 40-ton rotator shown here is a versatile response vehicle we use for loading equipment, accident recovery and heavy duty winching. We can respond to any situation you may encounter being the largest towing service in northern California. Visit us on the World Wide Web at greatamericatow.com.

Sound Tire is headquartered in Auburn, Washington with 7 other stores in Washington and Oregon. Its sister company is Coastal Tire Co. with 5 locations in Alaska. Sound Tire sells and services many of the largest Transportation, Construction, Mining, Utility and Private Carrier fleets in the Northwest. The Auburn Facility houses one of the most modern, technically advanced Bandag Retread facilities in the US. The company is an award winning supplier to these industries and conducts numerous seminars on topics such as driver training, maintenance process controls, and fleet management systems. The company is on the leading edge of modern fleet tire management. Visit Sound Tire on the World Wide Web at www.soundtire.com.

Nevada has been the fastest growing state in the country for the past several years, and Milne Tow and Transport's customers were having trouble finding an adequate on-demand supply of water trucks, lowbeds and dump trucks. Milne Tow and Transport has always had a large customer base of construction, mining and machinery supply customers, and promptly responded to their needs first with a couple of water trucks, then with an expanded complement of 15 for-hire construction trucks. This diversification in our equipment base has strengthened our relationship with our existing towing customers and allowed us to offer a more complete service with the same Milne assurance of quality and response.

See Following Page

More On Previous Page

Milne Tow and Transport has been a vital part of the transportation scene in Reno, Nevada since the late 1940's. The company's T.R.A.A. certified operators serve over 90,000 square miles of Nevada and California from 4 strategic locations. The economy of Nevada is highly dependent on courteous and friendly service to its visitors, and Milne is proud of its record of satisfied customers and community service. This photo of the famous Reno arch shows Milne's flagship, a T800 Kenworth equipped with a No-Mar T3035 recovery unit.

Mel Underwood Water Trucks, Inc. was started in 1970 by Mel Underwood and his wife Beverly with only one truck. Before Mel's death in 1991, their company's success had resulted in a fourteen truck fleet. Located in Sylmar, California, the business focuses on service to all motion picture companies. These services include wet downs for visual effects, rain shots and safety precautions for fire protection. We also supply various services to construction companies, county fire departments and the US Forest Service. All trucks in the Mel Underwood fleet are custom-built to exacting specifications. The company continues to grow due to the high level of satisfaction our customers experience and the resulting referrals.

Continued On Next Page

Continued From Previous Page

Here is Mel Underwood Water Truck's 4,000 gallon sprayer in action.

Stubbs Pro Tow of Lodi, California, has been a community fixture since the 1950's. The familiar motto, "Nobody pulls for you like the professionals at Stubbs," illustrates the training-oriented staff, and the photo selected below shows the range of their equipment. As the needs of the Sacramento/Lodi area have changed, owner Gary Guthrie has repositioned the company to handle everything from private tows to major eqiupment relocations. Gary himself has personally operated every piece of the equipment Stubbs owns, and the care and maintenance given to all units by their drivers reflects the pride felt company-wide.

Continued On Next Page

D iversity is the key to the survival of towing companies in the
1990's and beyond, and towing companies are finding that the
heavy haul and low bed business runs parallel to many aspects of
their heavy duty towing business. In many cases, low beds or
Landoll-type trailers are needed to transport damaged trucks and
trailers from accidents. Similarly, most heavy haul work runs with
little or no advance notice and fits into the flexible scheduling and
24-hour dispatching that full service towing companies such as
Stubbs already provide.

Continued From Next Page

2-speed 4.56/6.21 ratio rear axles. This truck was captured by HARCO's Manager Scott Palmer during an onsite move in Sparks, Nevada for Independent Construction Co. of Concord, CA. It is shown hauling a Caterpillar D10L dozer weighing 190,000 lbs, making the total gross weight of the vehicle combination of 267,000 lbs.

HARCO

Company was founded in 1970 and began its trucking operations in 1980 with one 10-wheel dump truck. HARCO Company has since grown into a fleet of 25 power units and some 75 trailers. Providing trucking service primarily in Northern Nevada and California, HARCO provides their loyal and expanding group of customers with professional and reliable service. This page shows their 1994 Peterbilt 379 with a Caterpillar 3406E 475 HP engine, 235" wheelbase and Fuller RTLO18718B 18-speed transmission. GCVW is 116,000 lbs and the overall length is 105 feet. Opposite is a 1995 Peterbilt 379 with a Caterpillar 3406E 475 HP engine, Fuller RTLO18718B 18-speed transmission, and Eaton DT461P

Continued On Previous Page

Milo's Towing got its start in 1957 when a friend suggested that AAA might be a good contract for the service station. Within 10 years, the low rates paid to the tow contractor had changed owner Milo Casagrande's mind about AAA, but not about towing as a business. By 1964, he had bought out a local company and entered the towing services market on all levels, light, medium and heavy duty. In 1979, the company moved to its new expanded location to serve the interstate, and it operates now as a full service mechanical repair facility for everything from the family wagon to big rigs. Milo's customer base has grown along with Montana and the operation is now managed by Gary Casagrande, Milo's son.

Teresi Trucking began operations with one truck in 1952. The company has grown gradually by fulfilling its customers' needs for quality service and specialized equipment. Teresi Trucking now operates an extensive fleet of late model power units and many types of specialized lowbed equipment as well as flatbeds and some vans. Much of the fleet is equipped with air ride suspension. Teresi's main traffic lanes are within the state of California but they also provide service to other western and southern states. The photo shows a sample of the many types of trailers that the company operates: a single drop lowbed, a 45' flatbed, a removable gooseneck lowbed and a double drop-stretch lowbed. Teresi Trucking believes that to provide superior service you need drivers that take pride in the job they do and the equipment they drive.

Michelis Trucking here presents truck 717, a 1987 Peterbilt model 359 extended hood with a 3406B ATA 425 HP Caterpillar engine. Truck 718 is a 1995 Peterbilt model 379 extended hood with a 3406A 400 HP Caterpillar engine. Both trucks featured here have RTO 14615 transmissions.

On The Cover

Michelis Trucking of Campbell, CA is the choice of the image-conscious electronics industry, and this 1988 Peterbilt model 379 with a 425 Caterpillar engine and a wheelbase of 328" with a 120" Double Eagle sleeper is kept busy running from the West Coast to Texas and back. The owner, Steve Michelis, specializes in transporting trade shows and electronics for Collins Transportation located since its establishment in 1980 by John Collins in Dallas, Texas. Starting with just one Peterbilt tractor in 1977, the company now owns 10 semi-end dump units, 8 transfer units and 6 bottom dump units, and a 20 year record of excellent service. Since 1980, Steve has had the pleasure of hauling for Central Concrete Supply Co., located in San José, CA.

Redfearn Trucking was founded in 1951 by Everett Redfearn. The company is a family owned and operated business. Don Redfearn is the president and CEO. The company is located in Stockton, California, and operates statewide. Some of their customers ar General Mills, Pillsbury and Carpenter Company. Redfearn's equipment reflects the image of its people. The tractor is a 1996 Freightliner, model FLB. The trailer is a 1996 53 foot "Strick" van with an aluminum floor.

The family wants to keep the business at its present size to give their customers 100% personalized service. Redfearn considers the twenty-one drivers and fifteen owner operators their most valubale asset. They have eighty 2 axle semi-trailers, mostly 53 foot vans.

Terry Johnson, owner of Terry Johnson Trucking, has been in business since 1979. The company's primary business is transporting road construction materials such as rock, sand, gravel and asphalt concrete. The company covers all of the state of California and parts of Nevada. Terry Johnson is the third generation of Johnsons to be in the business which originally started in the 1960's.

Terry has built his company from one truck in 1979 to almost 50 trucks at the present time. The fleet not only includes dump trucks, but also an assortment of construction equipment such as loaders, dozers, backhoes and heavy equipment hauling. The prime commodity of Terry Johnson Trucking is high quality service and hard work. These two attributes are the main reason for the growth and expansion of the company and planned future growth.

Owned and operated by Ted Hartman, the company got its start in 1986 with a single truck and refrigerated trailer operating in the northern states. Along with a desire to operate locally and a background in the construction industry, operations were shifted to dump trucks, and Ted Hartman Trucking began its present course.

Located in Puyallup, Washington, our customers are spread throughout the Puget Sound area of Western Washington, with occasional hauls to Oregon and Idaho. Ted's company motto is "You've got to love your work!" and that is evident in the appearance of the trucks and the quality of the work we do.

Ted drives one of the trucks, with 3 drivers employed to operate the other trucks. Credit the drivers with "loving their work", thus helping make us successful.

Technique Towing has sponsored this page for the Fresno Fire Department. The citizens and businesses of Fresno go about their work, play or rest hours secure in the knowledge that vehicles such as this 1979 American La France 1250 GPM two-stage pumper with more than 101,000 fire-fighting miles already on the clock are ready to swing into action at a moment's notice. Thanks to Chief Smith for allowing the time to photograph this one example of the city's fleet when it was being moved by Technique Towing.

Technique Towing of Fresno, California is a total service towing and recovery company with equipment ranging from light to heavy duty and air cushions for specialized recovery incidents. Clients include both private retail customers and commercial accounts such as motor clubs, dealerships, and municipal entities. Its Landoll trailer division serves a variety of clients with container, forklift and other non-automotive handling needs. Owners Steve and Marleen Rodgerson recently expanded operations to Oakhurst, 35 miles from the entrance to Yosemite National Park, and are establishing two additional locations to serve the Fresno and surrounding areas with minimum response times. "Credit our people," Steve states, "with our success. Their extra interest in the care of our customers has made the difference in our company."

McCarty and Sons Towing and Lowbed Service was started in 1976 by Bill McCarty with the help of his wife, Carol. In the very beginning they ran the business out of their home. In 1986, they began operating out of a facility in Oxnard, California, on the coast near the fast growing Port of Hueneme, one hour north of Los Angeles. McCarty & Sons was started as a towing company, but after buying a tractor and trailer to accomodate motorhomes and buses they expanded and now run numerous tractors and trailers. The company is growing rapidly and is committed to making changes to keep up with the current state of the business. Bill McCarty (President) is busy building up the interstate division, Carol oversees the office, their son Rod (Vice-President) is expanding the low-bed service division, and their son Brian (Vice-President) is in charge of the towing division, which all the family considers the heart of the business.

McCarty & Sons takes pride in their equipment because it is a reflection of the company. It lets their customers know that they will take pride in providing great service and fulfilling needs, which leads to loyal, long-term customers and friends. McCarty & Sons thanks their loyal customers and excellent employees for the company's success.

DenBeste Transportation was established in 1981 specializing in hazardous waste transportation, serving California and nine western states. The company has a fleet of 31 trailers, 14 power units and 300 hazardous waste roll off bins. The equipment shown on this page is a 1997 Peterbilt, series 379 with a 475 Caterpillar engine with a super 10 speed transmission a wheelbase of 260', 127" hood and 48' stand-up sleeper.

On the following page is a 1995 Peterbilt, series 379 with 475 Caterpillar, super 10 speed, 260" wheelbase and 60' sleeper, and a 1995 Peterbilt, series 379 with 475 Caterpillar, 18 speed transmission, two-speed Eaton rear ends, 230" wheelbase and 127" hood.

The trailers are a a 1991 Fruehauf 48x102 equipped with a double containment floor, 3,000 lb lift gate for the purpose of transporting waste drum loads and a 1997 PMF Semi Roll Off Unit with two 10,000 lb winches, one 40,000 winch, and spread axle air ride suspension capable of transporting two 18-yard hazardous waste containers, a 1990 Aluminum East trailer equipped with a roll over tarp system, air ride suspension, and barn door extra heavy floor to accommodate fork lift loading with a capacity of 60 yards.

Continued From Previous Page

Freddie Mac's of South El Monte, California, is celebrating 47 continuous years of business. Fred Meister, the "Freddie" of the company, used an Army vehicle and a chain to move a car out of the center of the street and that day, many years ago, Freddie Mac's was born. In the early 70's, the next generation got behind the wheel when, at 13 years old, son Danny got his first tow. Today Fred, Danny and Jeannie still run Freddie Mac's as a family operation. An all-Freightliner fleet of 45 technologically advanced tow trucks and 50 employees handle the everyday operations.

The original Fortier Transportation Co. was started in 1906 with horse drawn drayage wagons in Reedley, California. W.J. Fortier and R.A. Fortier built this company into a large diversified California carrier with over 200 power units and 6 freight terminals. This company was sold in 1960 to Ringsby Freight Lines. The name was reactivated in the late 1970's when it opened a charter bus company and some trucks. Ms. Ildiko (Kathy) Fortier is the owner and CEO of the current Fortier Transportation Co., a California statewide trucking carrier operating out of Fresno, offering vans, flats and pneumatic service.

Mike Lambert began driving a truck for his father Errol J. Lambert (d.b.a. Lambert & Son Trucking) in 1978, hauling quarry products in Watsonville, California, for Hildebrand & Son Trucking. In June of 1990, he bought his father out and started in business with his first custom glider kit, a 1987 Peterbilt Reliance transfer. Half of the fleet today hauls rock, sand and gravel, and the flatbed division handles everything from paper to agricultural products, ranging from Arizona to Oregon. Dawn Lambert, Mike's wife and the mother of their three children, has been his business partner from the start, doing the bookkeeping, dispatching, and myriad other tasks helping the company grow from one truck to eight. Here are two of the company's Peterbilts, a black 1997 and a red 1996. Both were custom built from glider kits by Mike, and both have 3406 Caterpillar engines, 10 speed transmissions and 11-24.5 low-pro tires. The brightest stars of the photo are Cole, Kim, and Kory, who were 12, 8 and 4 at the time of publication.

Dick's Wrecker Service of Medford, Oregon got its name from Dick Korner. In 1960, Maynard Hadley's Desert Service Towing merged its two trucks with Dick's and from that start the company grew to a fleet today of 28 units, with Maynard buying 6 other companies along the way. Along the I-5 corridor, routes 199, 99, 66 and 97 and in neighboring Ashland, Dick's serves as the police towing company and for 8 cities as well as county and state authorities. Drivers are T.R.A.A. and WreckMaster certified, the equipment is updated annually as towing technology changes, and the management of Dick's is undergoing a gradual transition from one generation to the next. On all company stationery appears the motto "Customer Satisfaction Guaranteed" and everyone's efforts strive toward that common goal.

Berry Brothers' familiar red and white trucks have been rescuing Oakland/San Francisco Bay area customers from mishaps, assisting with routine equipment movement, and serving as overall peace of mind for a large commercial and retail clientele since 1973. Towing and recovery is the company's core business, but owner Bob Berry believes strongly in professional training as an asset not only to his company but to Berry Brothers' colleagues in this difficult and often dangerous field. Well known nationally and statewide as a trainer in the field of heavy duty recovery, Bob is also active on the Board overseeing the establishment of the towing industry's first museum in Chattanooga, Tennessee.

An open invitation to visit the offices is extended to all, although it's not possible to guarantee a day as beautiful as the one on which this historic photograph was taken from Treasure Island.

This 1924 1-ton Model T truck restored to showroom quality is part of Rocha Transportation's fleet and is both a crowd-pleaser in parades and an award-winner at antique shows.

Continued on next page

Rocha Transportation's first truck was a milk truck bought in 1924 by Ed's father John. The company which began hauling cattle in 1935 today has grown to a super-modern fleet comprised of 50 power units and 75 sets of trailers. There are three tiers to the fleet with the top trucks hauling cattle, bulk wine and sugar. The second fleet handles containers and vans, and the third fleet runs freight products. Ed's wife, Carole, is the Office Manager and Doug, the third generation, is General Manager. A former President of the California Trucking Association, Ed Rocha is a strong advocate of rigorous safety inspections and though the trucks are kept in A-1 condition, they are sold after 5 or 6 years. This photo is a mini-fleet representing some of the types of trucks operated, taken at the Modesto, California, location.

Don Hickman Trucking, located in "The Cowboy Capitol Of The World," Oakdale, California, hauls a wide variety of materials including mushroom compost, crushed glass, limestone and various farm materials. Owned by Don and his partner/wife Marlene, this 1978 Peterbilt was bought by Don's family brand new and maintained by his brother and father before being passed to Don when his father retired in 1993. A full restoration gave the truck a new motor, Cummins big cam 400 blueprinted and balanced 13 speed transmission, SQ100 rear ends and all new drive lines. Jimmy "Pac Man" Paxia is the air brush artist responsible for the stunning graphics on the fuel tanks, drive lines, rear ends and motor. Don's Dad at 80 still keeps things humming.

GT Towing, owned by Garth and Linda Olson, got its start during a week of unusual wintry Seattle weather when Garth, just out of high school, watched a tow truck pull his beloved first car off after an accident. To pay off the bill, Garth worked for the garage and one day was told to "get in the tow truck and go get a car." Today, with mandatory CDL and other requirements, towing is a different business. GT Towing's small but diverse fleet operates in metropolitan Seattle and anywhere in Washington, towing any type of vehicle from loaded semi-tractors to low profile sports cars. The 1989 Peterbilt 379 shown here has a 400 Cummins engine, 35 ton Challenger boom and 25,000 axle lift, and was purchased specially for a contract awarded by the City of Seattle, Washington. It will, as Garth puts it, "handle it all".

KMD, Incorporated started in 1979 with three new trucks and 25 years of owner-operator experience. Cliff Moody and his wife Della built the company on the strength of careful attention to maintenance and putting driver comfort first. Having driven the 48 states for years, Cliff designed KMD to be so reliable, in terms of both its human capital and rolling stock, that its customers would respond with loyalty and the company would grow. With the help of his right hand man, Jerry Dennis, and children Lynn, Jim Ralph and Beth, and with the help of many quality employees, KMD did just that, growing to a fleet size of 100 power units and hauling for a wide variety of clients in the 11 western states.

Cliff's first solo trip to New York from Washington occurred when he was 12 years old, which his shocked mother discovered only after he had left. His father didn't see anything wrong with it, and neither did Cliff, so off he went, and that was the start of his long career. Although the company of the truck shown in this photo of the Seattle skyline ceased operations in 1996, the principles that made the company a standout for 20 years have kept some of the older trucks rock solid after multiple millions of miles of service. The image of this company helped set a professional tone for the trucking industry.

Southwest Crane and Rigging opened its doors in 1982, but its owner and driving force Harry Baker brought 15 years of previous experience to the company. Harry attributes the rapid growth since then to the team of experienced operators and managers which the company has attracted and then retained by fostering a can-do work environment. Today the transportation and heavy haul division runs locally as well as throughout the Southwest including Mexico. The all-hydraulic fleet of cranes can service the smallest lifts and the biggest, with up to 300 Ton capacity and 365 feet of reach. Forklifts from 5,000 to 80,000 lb capacity complete the equipment list. Visit our headquarters in Phoenix, or call for more information 602/256-7161.

Bed Rock, Inc. of Point Arena, California is owned by Bill, Karen, Richard and Bob Hay, and is the result of years of hard work and family participation by all including Stacy and Missy. In 1986, after 20 years building a group of successful businesses ranging from ranching to the building of 5 coastal sub-divisions, Bed Rock, Inc. was born. Sons Richard and Bob, having graduated from high school in 1985 and 1988 and completed college, joined the company as owners. From a couple of trucks, the company has grown to a fleet of 17 trucks today, competing each year in various competitions in California and Nevada, always taking First Place Awards including Highway Patrol Awards. The company has 18 employees, and the rock

Continued On Next Page

Continued From Previous Page

quarry enterprise allows Bed Rock. Inc. to offer complete construction services from base rock to foundation forms, road pioneering to asphalt surfaces. Bed Rock, Inc. proudly serves the Northern Sonoma/Southern Mendocino County coast with quality construction materials and site development equipment. The 1987 Peterbilt shown was purchased in 1994. Following their usual custom, the sons stripped the truck and Bill painted it. Fancy chrome and special wheels were added, and Fred "The Brush" Daily added his one-of-a-kind murals on each door, accented with gold leaf. Bill and Karen visited the J & L factory in Texas and added to the cement bulk trailer 132 lights to outline the whole trailer. Both units assembled stretch a full 75' and travel up and down the narrow, winding Highway 1 roads along the northern coastline of California.

Bob and Melisa Pearce, owners of Synergistic Transportation, have been doing business in Phoenix, Arizona, since 1989. With a dedicated fleet of 13 stainless steel tankers, their specialty is hauling liquid food grade sweeteners. For power units, Synergistic Transportation has leases with four very talented Owner-Operators, while operating one company-owned tractor. This 1997 Kenworth W900L is Bob's personal tractor, powered by a 3406E 550 HP Caterpillar with an 18 speed transmission. The trailer is a 1997 Brenner stainless steel food grade tank with a capacity of 4,500 gallons.

Oak Harbor Freight Lines, Inc. was started by Ben Koetje in 1916, and has changed family hands only once since: in 1936 for the sum of $600. Today, under the guidance of the second Vander Pol generation and building on the solid foundation of the first, Oak Harbor's operations have spread from Oak Harbor, WA, into first Oregon, and then Nevada, Idaho and California. Over a short 10-year period this expansion was accomplished along with the construction of modern terminals and establishment of advanced computerized management information systems. The foresighted institution of Quality Process as a company-wide operations philosophy has resulted in steadily better and more competitive customer service, which Oak Harbor took full advantage of while surviving the price wars of 1995. Emerging with strong, new eastbound partnerships firmly in place, the company looks forward to the new millennium with confidence.

B & B Red-i-Mix
Mike Gatherer
590 Live Oak
Irwindale, CA 91706-1315
Tel: 800/700-8371
Fax: 818/359-0541

Bed Rock, Inc.
Bill and Karen Hay
P.O. Box 366
Point Arena, CA 95468
Tel: 707/882-2323
Fax: 707/882-3258

Berkeley Concrete Pumping
Steve Pryde
1200 6th Street
Berkeley, CA 94710
Tel: 510/525-4111
Fax: 510/527-0782

Berry Brothers
Bob Berry
598 55th Street
Oakland, CA 94609
Tel: 800/464-7215
Fax: 510/653-3263

Bill & Wags, Inc.
Bill Robertson
1516 S. Bon View Avenue
Ontario, CA 91761-4407
Tel: 909/923-6100
Fax: 909/923-6108

Black Gold Industries
Victor Villard
527 N. Rice Avenue
Oxnard, CA 93030-8924
Tel: 805/981-4616
Fax: 805/981-0105

C.T.I., Inc.
Terry Fortier
P.O. Box 12004
Fresno, CA 93776
Tel: 209/275-0444
Fax: 209/276-9267

Denbeste Transportation, Inc.
Lorie & Bill Denbeste
930 Shiloh Rd #44
Windsor, CA 95492
Tel: 707/838-1407
Fax: 707/838-7947

Dick's Wrecker
Maynard Hadley
4048 Crater Lake Avenue
Medford, OR 97504
Tel: 541/772-4040
Fax: 541/779-1818

Don Hickman Trucking
Don Hickman
PO Box 2336
Oakdale, CA 95361
Tel: 209/848-8952
Fax: 209/848-2565

Double Eagle
Jerry Butcher
14039 Santa Ana Avenue
Fontana, CA 92337
Tel: 909/428-3770
Fax: 909/428-3773

Doug Andrus Distributing, Inc.
Doug and Heber Andrus
1820 West Broadway
Idaho Falls, ID 83402
Tel: 208/523-1034
Fax: 208/522-7947

Fortier Transportation
Kathy Fortier
3449 West Franklin
Fresno, CA 93706
Tel: 800/411-7210
Fax: 209/275-0626

Freddie Mac's, Inc.
Fred Meister
2740 N. Bruin Avenue
South El Monte, CA 91733
Tel: 818/443-4141
Fax: 818/444-6704

Ganduglia Trucking
Jim Ganduglia
4746 East Florence Ave
Fresno, CA 93725
Tel: 209/251-7101
Fax: 209/251-5479

GREAT AMERICA TOW & TRANSPORT
DINO TOMASSI
560 E. GISH ROAD
SAN JOS , CA 95112
TEL: 408/283-8571
FAX: 408/287-3184

GT TOWING
GARTH AND LINDA OLSON
3252 HARBOR AVENUE
SEATTLE, WA 98126
TEL: 206/938-4423
FAX: 206/935-9849

HARCO COMPANY
SCOTT PALMER
601 CHENEY STREET
RENO, NV 89502
TEL: 702-329-7089
FAX: 702/329-5932

HARRIS RANCH
MANNY DE LA OSSA
ROUTE 1 BOX 400
COALINGA, CA 93210
TEL: 209/884-2435
FAX: 209/884-2253

HASTIE'S CAPITOL SAND & GRAVEL
RANDY HASTIE
9350 JACKSON RD
SACRAMENTO, CA 95826
TEL: 800/427-3867
FAX: 916/361-2441

HAYS OLD TRUCK TOWN MUSEUM
DON AND NAOMI HAYS
2000 EAST MAIN STREET
WOODLAND, CA 95776
TEL: 916/666-1044
FAX: 916/668-5890

JOEL OLSON TRUCKING
JOEL AND CAROLE OLSON
17901 BEAVER FALLS RD P.O. BOX 837
CLATSKANIE, OR 97016
TEL: 360/694-8610
FAX: 503/728-3319

KELVIN HILDEBRAND, INC.
KELVIN HILDEBRAND
6 LEWIS ROAD
WATSONVILLE, CA 95076
TEL: 408/449-1521
FAX: 408/722-0658

KINGS COUNTY TRUCK LINES
MANUEL MANCEBO, JR.
754 S. BLACKSTONE
TULARE, CA   93275
TEL: 800/842-5285
FAX: 209/687-8446

KMD, INC.
LYNN DENNIS
401 LUND ROAD
AUBURN, WA 98002
TEL: 800/275-5634
FAX: 206/939-7795

LAMBERT TRUCKING
MIKE AND DAWN LAMBERT
P.O. BOX 1528
WATSONVILLE, CA 95076
408/722-6083

MAGGINI HAY CO. INC.
MELVIN MAGGINI
5350 W. MT. WHITNEY
RIVERDALE, CA 93656
TEL: 209/867-4338
FAX: 209/867-3891

MCCARTY & SONS TOWING & LOWBED SERVICE
BILL AND CAROL MCCARTY
1608 E. 5TH STREET
OXNARD, CA 93031
TEL: 805/487-0117
FAX: 805/486-3213

MEL UNDERWOOD WATER TRUCKS, INC.
BEVERLY UNDERWOOD
13201 FOOTHILL BLVD.
SYLMAR, CA 91352-4832
TEL: 818/361-9176
FAX: 818/361-9617

MICARELLI TRUCKING
TOM AND SHIRLEY MICARELLI
639 MANZANITA DRIVE
FILLMORE, CA 93015
TEL: 805/524-0125
FAX: 805/524-0125

MICHELIS TRUCKING
STEVE MICHELIS
478 WEST HAMILTON #274
CAMPBELL, CA 95008
TEL: 408/288-6722
FAX: 408/288-6796

MID-STATE TRUCKING & RIGGING
DICK BAKER
2650 N. 32ND AVENUE
PHOENIX, AZ 85009
TEL: 602/278-6281
FAX: 602/278-5191

MILNE TOW SERVICE
GENE TEMEN
1700 MARIETTA WAY P.O. BOX M
SPARKS, NV 89432
TEL: 800/323-4665
FAX: 702/359-0155

MILO'S TOWING & REPAIR
MILO CASAGRANDE
200 CENTENNIAL
BUTTE, MT 89701
TEL: 406/723-4140
FAX: 406/723-9208

MP ENVIRONMENTAL SERVICES
GINA BLANKENSHIP
3400 MANOR STREET
BAKERSFIELD, CA 93308
TEL: 805/393-1151
FAX: 805/393-3834

OAK HARBOR FREIGHT LINES INC.
EDWARD VANDER POL
1225 37TH STREET NW
AUBURN, WA 98071-1469
TEL: 800/285-6254
FAX: 206/931-5137

PASO ROBLES DIESEL
STEVE ORMONDE
P.O. BOX 2053
PASO ROBLES, CA 93446
TEL: 805/238-1466
FAX: 805/238-5189

PAYTON TRUCKING
CARL BATES
3330 S. PRATT AVENUE
TULARE, CA 93274
TEL: 209/688-6292
FAX: 209/688-4735

REDFEARN TRUCKING INC.
DON REDFEARN
P.O. BOX 5503
STOCKTON, CA 95205
TEL: 209/948-0080
FAX: 209/465-6104

RESOURCE MATERIAL INC.
P.O. BOX 5267
BUENA PARK, CA 90620
TEL: 714/952-2993
FAX: 714/952-2710

ROCHA TRANSPORTATION
ED ROCHA
319 E. WHITMORE AVE.
MODESTO, CA 95358
TEL: 209/538-1302
FAX: 209/538-6302

SOUND TIRE, INC.
KIM LORENZ
402 LUND RD. P.O. BOX 10
AUBURN, WA 98071-0010
TEL: 206/941-6100
FAX: 206/833-5661

SOUTHWEST INDUSTRIAL RIGGING
HARRY BAKER
218 WEST WATKINS ROAD
PHOENIX, AZ 85003
TEL: 602/256-7161
FAX: 602/256-7171

STUBBS PRO TOW
GARY GUTHRIE
400 N. CLUFF AVENUE
LODI, CA 95240
TEL: 209/368-9855
FAX: 209/369-8878

SWARD TRUCKING, INC.
VIC AND GAIL SWARD
P.O. BOX 8
OAKDALE, CA 95361
TEL: 209/847-4218
FAX: 209/847-3725

Synergistic Transportation
Robert Pearce
448 South 11th Avenue
Phoenix, AZ 85007
TEL: 602/254-6175
FAX: 602/256-7845

Technique Towing
Steve Rodgerson
2495 N. Miami
Fresno, CA 93727
TEL: 209/291-3262
FAX: 209-291-3237

Ted Hartman Trucking
Ted Hartman
16904 85th Avenue E
Puyallup, WA 98373
TEL: 206/840-2844

Teresi Trucking Inc.
A. Todd Teresi
P.O. Box 1270
Lodi, CA 95241
TEL: 800/692-3431
FAX: 209/369-2830

Terry Johnson Trucking
Dee Johnson
31186 West Gale
Coalinga, CA 93210
TEL: 209/935-3231
FAX: 209/935-5803

Valley Materials
Lloyd Farmer
161 E. Transportation
French Camp, CA 95231
TEL: 209/469-4803
FAX: 209/982-5126

West Coast Sand & Gravel
John Struiksma
7312 Orangethorne Avenue PO Box 5267
Buena Park, CA 90620
TEL: 714/522-5780
FAX: 714/522-4524